If I Only Knew

First-Time Bestselling Authors Reveal Insider Secrets to Writing a Book

If I Only Knew

First-Time Bestselling Authors
Reveal Insider Secrets to
Writing a Book

Phoenix, Arizona

Laura Bush, PhD
and Sarah Bush Lloyd

If I Only Knew: First-Time Bestselling Authors Reveal Insider Secrets to Writing a Book

Copyright © 2018 by Laura Bush, PhD, and Sarah Bush Lloyd

First Published in the USA in 2018 by Peacock Proud Press, Phoenix, Arizona
First Edition

ISBN 978-0-9993675-6-8 paperback
ISBN 978-0-9993675-7-5 eBook

Lbrary of Congress Control Number: 2018956846

Editor:
Laura Bush, PhD, PeacockProud.com

Interior Layout:
Melinda Tipton Martin, MartinPublishingServices.com

Cover Design:
FuturePhotoGroup.com

DISCLAIMER:
This is a work of nonfiction. The information is of a general nature to help readers know and understand more about writing and publishing a book. Readers of this publication agree that Laura Bush, PhD, Sarah Bush Lloyd, and any authors included and named in this book will not be held responsible or liable for damages that may be alleged or resulting directly or indirectly from their use of this publication. All external links are provided as a resource only and are not guaranteed to remain active for any length of time. The authors cannot be held accountable for the information provided by, or actions resulting from accessing these resources.

CONTENTS

PART II: BONUS
Information and Guidance from Experts / 51

CHAPTER 6
Three Big Barriers to Writing a Bestselling Book / 53

CHAPTER 7
Debunking the Myth of the Lone Writer / 59

CHAPTER 8
Writing an Autobiography that Leaves a Lasting Legacy / 65

CHAPTER 9
Choosing the Best Transcription Services / 71

Chapter 10
Three Ways to Find Time to Write / 75

CHAPTER 11
Is Your Editor a Friend or Foe? / 79

CHAPTER 12
Why You, Too, Are Good Enough to Write Your Book / 83

CHAPTER 13
Financing Your Writing / 87

CHAPTER 14

CHAPTER 15

CONCLUSION

Becoming a First-Time Author

If I Only Knew: First-Time Bestselling Authors Reveal Insider Secrets to Writing a Book recognizes that authors who are new to writing a book share some (or all) of the following legitimate questions, fears, and concerns:

- I've always wanted to write a book, but I don't know where to start.

- I'm worried that I stink at grammar and that I don't know how to write well enough to become the author of a book.

- I'm afraid people won't read my book, or, if they *do* read it, they'll be critical of my ideas.

- I stop myself from writing because I don't know how I'll publish my book, even if I do finish writing it.

Do you recognize yourself in any of these statements? If you answered, "Yes," then the insider secrets and advice you'll get from these first-time authors will quiet your fears, answer many of your questions, and show you how you, too, can courageously move forward to experience benefits you can't foresee, even beyond the immediate thrill of publishing your book.

At Peacock Proud Press, we started interviewing our first-time authors about what they wish they had known before they wrote their first book for two reasons. First, we believed that finding out what other first-time authors wish they had known *before* they started writing could help inform and jumpstart other would-be authors on their own book writing journey. Second, we wanted to learn from what our authors told us to help improve our own writing, editing, and publishing services for future clients. (Based on our interviews, for example, we have begun developing a detailed overview and timeline for authors that previews our assisted self-publishing process.)

Part I: Insider Secrets from First-Time Authors

In Part I of this book, the unique perspective and insider secrets first-time authors share about writing their book—the trials *and* the triumphs—will show you that it IS possible to finish YOUR book and that the outcomes from publishing a book can be bigger than you even imagine. But fair warning: one thing these authors all have in common is that writing their first book has motivated them to start writing a *second* book!

You should also know that these first-time authors did not write their books alone. After reading their insider secrets, we hope you'll come to realize that authoring a book that people buy, read, and recommend is not something you do on your own. Look at the acknowledgments page of any well-written book for proof that writing a book is not a solitary act. Instead, these authors wrote their books with the help of mentors, friends, family members, partners, spouses, and other supporters. In addition, they relied on the expertise of an experienced writing coach, editor, and publisher, Dr. Laura Bush.

Part II: BONUS Information and Guidance from Experts

In Part II of this book, you'll get BONUS chapters with practical information and guidance from Dr. Bush and her team of experts to help you find time to write, work with an editor, finance your writing, choose a publisher, and much more. By answering your questions and concerns at many stages during the writing, editing, and publishing process, Dr. Bush and her team share the most vital knowledge you need to fulfill your own dream of publishing a book. At Peacock Proud Press, we encourage you to identify and hire the right team to support you in getting your book out in the world, so that you, too, can share your message and make the difference you want to make.

Insider Secrets from First-Time Authors

CHAPTER 1

Aaron Anderson
American Kundalini

In his late thirties, Aaron experienced Kundalini (universal energy)—a decade long event that radically transformed his life. To make sense of this unusual experience, Aaron turned to his long-time mentor, a respected religious studies scholar, Dr. Kenneth Morrison. Together, they plotted a course to better understand Kundalini through rigorous self-examination and empirical experimentation. Aaron's memoir, *American Kundalini*, is the culmination of lessons carefully learned from his first-hand experience living with Kundalini in a modern context. Aaron is an award-winning architect who currently resides in San Diego.

Sample of Accomplishments after Publishing *American Kundalini*

- Eckhart Tolle "liked" *American Kundalini* on Instagram, May 8, 2018.

- Aaron wrote an Epilogue and is releasing a second edition of his first book.

- Two years later, Aaron has finished writing his second book.

Aaron's Insider Secrets for First-Time Authors

When I started writing my first book, *American Kundalini: One Westerner's Unexpected Journey with Universal Energy* (December 2016), I really had no expectations about the project. I wasn't thinking, "Oh, I'm going to write a book." The idea came out of an organic relationship I had with Laura Bush, and I just started doing it. Also, in my family, we already had a writer who was known as "the" writer, so it was surprising when I became a writer in the family, too!

Be willing to be honest and vulnerable—not perfect.

I would tell new writers, "You can't freak out about being vulnerable or your book won't resonate with people. You have to be honest in your writing." I also know there are parts of my book that aren't perfect because Laura edited them, and I changed a few of her edits back. She never insisted that her edits remain. Perfectionism is not the goal. We aren't trying to be perfect writers. People don't expect that. If you try to be perfect, you may never get started, let alone finish, and then people may never have your book to read. People just want to hear the story.

You might be amazed at how quickly your book comes together.

A book takes time and commitment, but once I started, I slowed down on my work as an architect and put more time into writing. The concept of writing a book is foreign to most of us non-writers. I don't think any of us think our writing skills are good enough, but once you're into the writing, you realize, this isn't so bad.

I think the best part about writing my book was that it became doable—not monumental or not like a mountain too hard to climb. I wrote for exactly one year with Laura coaching me and editing the manuscript. A month and a half later, my book was designed and available on Amazon. Now, two years later, I've written an Epilogue describing what has happened for me on my journey with Kundalini since I published the book in 2016. It will be re-published in a second edition.

Trust the creative process. Not knowing everything beforehand can be a good thing.

It was probably a good thing that I didn't know everything about the process of writing a book and getting it published because I could have been overwhelmed and that could have shut down my creative process.

There was this disconnect I experienced between the creative process I wanted to stay in and the technical aspects of publishing a book. I saw Laura's expertise with editing and publishing as protecting me from embarrassment because I could get lost in the process of writing such personal things. I just told myself, "Let Laura take care of all of that!" It's nice to have someone be logical to protect you when you're in "emotional mode."

Do yourself a favor and hire a writing coach.

My book is autobiographical. I needed someone like Laura because I was writing something very personal, and yet it was going to become very public. As a first-time writer, I was not totally confident in the story I was telling, particularly because I wasn't a professional writer. I wondered, "Is my story just interesting to me or will it be interesting to other people?"

Laura didn't have a preconceived notion of what my book should be. She really let me tell the story in my own voice. Then she gave me the confidence to know that the story I was telling about my personal experience would be worthwhile for others to hear. You will do yourself a favor by hiring a coach who can give you immediate, unbiased feedback.

She also took my story and made it relatable. She helped the story make sense, stay on track, and not go off on tangents—

so nothing took away from the core story. As an editor, she trimmed things up and made the book cohesive. I wish I could find the words to say what an amazing experience it is to work with Laura. I felt at ease. I just can't say enough about her.

Try handwriting your first draft rather than typing on a computer.

Most people will type their book on the computer, but I have to say, for the second book I'm writing, I've handwritten it. I think my writing has actually gone quicker because when I type on the computer, I constantly stop typing to edit, rather than just write it all out and *then* go back and edit. I'd encourage you to consider handwriting your first draft rather than typing everything on your computer.

Like anything, you get what you pay for.

In my profession as an architect, people determine what kind of architect they want to hire. Certain architects are associated with a higher quality structure, and if they are, then as a prospective client of that architect, you realize you will have to spend more money to hire them. In regard to writing your book, you might ask yourself, "What can I live with or what can I not live without? What caliber of editor, book designer, and publisher do I want to hire?" You're going to have to spend more money to get quality. Writing a professional book comes with a cost. I think I probably put ten grand into my book. I'm not saying that's high at all. But you have to be realistic about what writing and publishing a great book takes.

Ultimately, you choose how much you want to spend. I think it's important to say that I had the control NOT to spend $10,000. I could have spent $5,000, but the book wouldn't have been the quality I wanted. I wouldn't have had the amount of time Laura spent with me personally if I had only spent $5,000. I would also have given up certain things, like a great cover, but I knew I'd be looking at this book the rest of my life! Now that the book is published, I'm carrying it around and giving it to EVERY person I know—and more! I'm glad I feel great when I hand my book to someone.

Use an actual book designer.

Toward the end, I thought, "Well, I'm a designer, so to save money, I can do the book cover design myself." I was totally wrong about that. I'm thrilled with my book designer, Melinda Tipton Martin. She works with Laura's authors and has her own book design business.

Book designing is like the metaphor that even a good surgeon can't do surgery on him or herself. For me, it was weird, because with my architecture, I do very modern, contemporary, clean designs. I saw some of the covers my designer, Melinda, had created in her online portfolio. She lives in Texas and didn't really do modern stuff, but she came up with the perfect modern book cover over night! Now I know I couldn't design my own book cover. I'm too close to my book, and I'm not a professional book designer either.

If the cover of a book is thoughtful, then the book is probably thoughtful too.

In architecture, they say you sell the "sizzle not the steak." So that's how people buy a book, too, because they don't know the meat of the story. It's the aesthetics of the cover that make a difference about whether they will buy and read your book or not. I believe that if the book cover is thoughtful, the book is probably thoughtful too.

How to Contact Aaron Anderson

Book Website

americankundalini.com

Professional Website

studio-anderson.com

Social Media

instagram.com/studioandersonarchitecture/

Email

aaron@studio-anderson.com

CHAPTER 2

Meina J. Dubetz
When Death Comes Knocking for Your Patients

Meina J. Dubetz was born in the Netherlands and im-migrated with her parents to Calgary, Alberta, Canada at age three. When she was seventeen, Meina began working in a nursing home during the summer where she discovered her passion for caring for patients facing the end of their lives. This experience paved the way for her to become a Licensed Practical Nurse and then later fulfill her dream to become a Registered Nurse. With over thirty years of oncology nursing experience in both in-patient and out-patient settings, Meina's connection with her patients, their families, and her peers continue to move and inspire her.

Sample of Accomplishments after Publishing
When Death Comes Knocking for Your Patients

- Regularly asked to speak. Example speaking invitations: Mount Royal University, Canadian Brain Tumor Foundation Professional Health Care Symposium, Apr. 2018; Vancouver Health Care Professionals' Symposium and Canadian Brain Tumor Foundation, May 2018; Canadian Palliative Care Conference, Sep. 2018.

- Book reviewed and named "Book of the Month" by the International Association for Hospice and Palliative Care, July 2018.

- Over 14,500 followers attained on LinkedIn since the book's publication.

Meina's Insider Secrets for First-Time Authors

Before I started writing my book, *When Death Comes Knocking for Your Patients: A Guide for Nurses and Palliative Caregivers* (September 2017), I wish I had known that I *am* a good writer. I did not realize that. It was always my passion to write, but I never felt good enough. It wasn't until I started writing that I realized I had an ability that surprised me. Dr. Laura told me, "You are a really good storyteller!" It took someone like her, with a PhD in English, to make me believe in myself and move me past my own doubts.

Don't let self-doubt hold you back or slow you down.

It took me two and a half years to write my first book, but I could have written it faster if I wouldn't have let self-doubt hold me back. At some point, Laura got straight with me and said, "You know what? This book is really needed and you need to make a difference for other people! That's what you *want* to do, and you're the one to do it!"

As my writing coach, Laura saw that I was making any excuse not to cross the finish line. I kept putting the brakes on, telling myself I was just taking my time writing this book. She was graceful to give me time, but then it got to the point where she asked, "What is stopping you?" That's when it got real.

Her persistence pushed me through to finish with confidence, which was always there underneath the self-doubt.

Your real-world experience matters.

If I had known how successful my book was going to be, I would have written it faster! Instead, I thought, "What do I know? In nursing, we've got people who have their PhD's." Finally, I realized I didn't have to have a PhD to write a book. My thirty years of on-the-ground experience as an oncology nurse gave me the ability to write my book.

It was my own story in my own head that had me think this book wouldn't be well-received. With supportive coaching, I learned I AM an authority! I AM an authority on my own life! And that's what I was writing about. Nobody can take that away.

Your book could make a much bigger impact than you realize.

My book went #1 on Amazon in the USA and Canada. After its publication, Pima Medical School in Phoenix, Arizona adopted the book for fifty seniors in its nursing program, one of the largest in the nation. Who would have thought? Since publishing, I've also had amazing opportunities to speak and have done two national conferences in Canada just in the last month. I've been asked to do another conference this fall. I've also been asked to do workshops and talks at institutions like hospitals, cancer centers, and retirement homes. Some of these institutions pay all my expenses, and they give me an opportunity to promote my book.

When I'm speaking, I read an excerpt so people get a sample of what my book is about. Then they purchase my book or tell other people about it (word of mouth promotion), which is the whole reason I wrote the book—to make a difference by sharing my knowledge to help educate those who are caring for people who are dying.

Since publishing the book, I now have 14,500 followers on LinkedIn! I probably get about ten requests a day to speak, including at international conferences. At least 80 percent of the requests are from people who would benefit from my book, but at this point, the speaking supports them more than it supports me financially. I'm not looking at these invitations as, "Oh, they just want me for nothing." I'm looking at these invitations as a sign from the universe of what is to come, including a recent development to have my book translated into Spanish.

Speaking is just like having a conversation.

One thing that surprised me is how confident I feel as a speaker. I have no nervousness getting up in front of people to speak. I believe it's because I'm speaking from my heart, and this is a message I want to get across. Speaking is no different than having a one-on-one conversation. Why would I feel nervous talking to a group of people that I'm just having a conversation with? We can all learn from each other. I don't have anything I need to prove. When I speak at a conference or hold a workshop, I simply want to find out what more my audience wants to know, or how I can help them make more of a difference in the work they are doing.

Invest in yourself. Allow others to support and invest in you.

I was amazed at the amount of people that had my back to get this book done. I thought an author's journey would be one that I had to travel on my own. I know the people that love me and support me made the journey easier, and I didn't feel like I was doing it on my own. I'm especially fortunate that I had my husband's full support. He was the one that said, "You need to go with Laura." If I had been left to my own devices, I think I would have struggled. My husband saw what a great book I was writing, and he felt it was worth investing in me.

I also got financial support from my mom. She gifted me the money to go to the "Book in a Barn" writing retreat that Laura holds in Arizona. I didn't value myself enough to believe I could invest in myself to attend a writing retreat—but my mother did. Without her, my husband, and many other people's encouragement, I might still be unpublished!

Attend a writing retreat with like-minded people and get positive feedback.

I think the energy of like-minded people writing together at the "Book in a Barn" retreat sparked me. It lit up my dream of being published. I had the support I needed to get my book finished by talking with people who listened to my writing and gave me positive feedback. Participating in a writing retreat firmed up the belief that my dream could be a reality. It also got me organized to see where to go after the retreat.

At "Book in a Barn," there's a place for everybody at any stage in their writing process: those almost finished with their writing, those who have a baseline for what they want to write, and those just starting, but not sure where to go.

Ask for support.

Asking for help is difficult. Enroll people in what you want to do around your book, so that they hear you as a future author, which creates the opportunity for you to share with them what is standing in your way. Then watch the support come in. I don't think you can just go up to somebody and say, "Hey, I'm writing this book, and I really need $5,000." What you can do is enroll the person into the idea of the book, have him or her see the difference your published book can make, and then watch the miracles of money come in to make your dream come true.

You'll probably discover you want to write more books.

Lastly, I am surprised to KNOW I have another book in me. In fact, I have several more books in me. I'm visualizing the next book to be, *When Death Comes Knocking for Your Parishioners* as a support for spiritual leaders. I've learned that a lot of seminary training doesn't delve much into what really happens as a person with a terminal illness is dying.

I imagine a series of books: *When Death Comes Knocking for Siblings* or *When Death Comes Knocking for Parents*. What I would love to have is people contribute their experiences to these books because I think it is therapeutic to tell your own stories of what it's like to lose someone. Those stories can empower people who have gone through loss or are facing "Death's Knock."

Give your book to a company you trust who knows self-publishing.

I am grateful that I did not try to self-publish my book on my own—you know, find this person to do the editing and that person to do the designing or the printing, because I know my book would still be unpublished. To be able to place my book in the hands of somebody like Laura, who knows what she's doing and who was as passionate about having my book published as I was myself, I knew it was in safe hands and that it would be taken care of.

I did what I know how to do—write the book. I am not a publisher. Give your book to somebody that is. My son published a book, and he had used Laura to do the editing. When I talked about writing my book he said, "Mom, you have to contact Laura." There was no doubt in my mind. I knew her life has integrity and I trusted her.

How to Contact Meina J. Dubetz

Book website

meinadubetz.com

Social Media

linkedin.com/in/meina-dubetz/
facebook.com/AuthorMeinaDubetz/

Email

meina@meinaDubetz.com

CHAPTER 3

Rhonda Willford Eberst
I Survived Pompeii

Rhonda Willford Eberst is passionate about turning kids on to reading. Raised in Wyoming, she moved to Ohio with her husband and has been with the Reynoldsburg City Schools for twenty years. Rhonda is an author, humorist, and speaker. She currently serves as the Librarian and Director of the Summit STEM Living Library Museum where she plays for a living.

Sample of Accomplishments after Publishing
I Survived Pompeii

- Approximately one hundred people attended Rhonda's book signing launch in Ohio.

- In less than one hour, she sold out forty books at a book signing hosted by Barnes & Noble in Pickerington, Ohio.

- Columbus, Ohio School District bought 151 books and hired Rhonda to speak in fall 2018 to their librarians and administrators, the official launch of her new speaking career.

Rhonda's Insider Secrets for First-Time Authors

Before writing my book, *I Survived Pompeii: Hilarious Adventures in an Elementary School Library* (March 2018), I wish I had known more about the writing process and how to use programs like MS Word. That would have saved me a lot of editing time, but hiring a writing coach like Laura to teach me these things went beyond improving my grammar. Her coaching made a big difference in my ability to know what I wanted to say—and who I was actually writing to. I discovered I couldn't just be "out there telling stories." To be effective, I had to hone into writing for a specific person—a specific audience.

Be adaptable and coachable when revising, especially with multiple drafts.

I'm old fashioned. My former typing teacher, Mrs. Wimberly, told us "two spaces after a period," so at my age, it was challenging to learn new rules for writing. Also, my tenses were all over the place. I didn't even think about the need to decide what tense (past or present) to use for my stories.

I would tell new writers not to take coaching and editing personally. When I first hired Laura, I gave her what I thought was a final draft. It turns out, that draft was nowhere near a final draft! In fact, it wasn't even close! First-time writers need to be adaptable and coachable when revising.

Ask for an overview of the publishing process.

I know Laura didn't want to overwhelm me, but a detailed overview of the publishing process would have helped me: this is my team; this is what they are going to do; this is how this works; this is the kind of time it takes. Then, once it's out of your hands and into your publishing team's hands, you have to be patient as an author, and you may be given other assignments. An overview would have helped me because I didn't even know what a "CreateSpace" account was or why I would use it. I just knew my book was going to be print-on-demand on Amazon.

Research and budget for costs to publish and launch a book.

As a first-time author, you probably have no idea what it costs to write, publish, and launch a book and, for me, launch a speaking career, too. I wish I had had a stronger sense of what to budget for, even before starting to write. The $5,000 my husband and I initially allotted for editing and publishing was only the beginning. For example, you will need to budget for ordering the book for your in-person book launch event(s), to pay for a website, and to invest in marketing materials (I created personalized bookmarks and 4 x 6 inch cards to publicize my speaking). Research what else you might need, so you can save early on and budget for those costs.

Invest in a trusted coach, editor, and publishing company that wants to build a relationship with you, not just make money.

Some people believe they can publish a book on their own. I could have published on my own, but my book would not have been anything like it is today. I would not have the cover I have. I would not have known how to launch a book. But most of all, the substance of the book would never have compared to what my book is now. Investing in an independent book publishing company like Peacock Proud Press is critical if you want to get a quality product.

Laura has the ability to build trusting relationships with people. I looked at another publishing place and talked to this gentleman for quite a while before I approached Laura at Peacock Proud Press. The other publisher was offering 50 percent off and quite a few things that Peacock Proud Press offers, but if something sounds too good to be true, it probably is. I knew the coaching wasn't going to be there. I just knew I wouldn't have a relationship with the man I spoke to. He was a salesman. He wasn't interested in building a relationship with me or teaching me what Laura taught me. The coaching was missing, and great coaching is a really big deal!

Afterwards, I heard about some books this man published. There were many complaints, and authors weren't getting their money from royalties of the book. He had told me, "You can count on earning $2.00 per book." Also, his company would have taken the manuscript I sent him and published it just the way it was. When I gave my manuscript to Laura, she did not see it as a final draft. She saw how it could be improved, so my first draft was really the beginning of several more drafts with several more edits.

Laura wants writers to really write as themselves, to be passionate about their subject matter—not just write for money. When you work with a publisher like Peacock Proud Press, you are doing something to contribute to humanity. That's Laura's value system—the world she loves. She doesn't want to just be an English teacher who puts marks on a paper. She coaches a writer like me who will make a difference for the masses because she wants her company to make a difference in the world. If you want to write a book just to make money, don't use Laura as a coach. She wants to work with people who are passionate about something and want to make a difference for other people.

How to Contact Rhonda Willford Eberst

Website

rhondawilfordeberst.com

Social Media

facebook.com/AuthorRhondaWillfordEberst/

linkedin.com/in/rhondawillfordeberst/

Email

rhonda@rhondawilfordeberst.com

reberst@reyn.org

CHAPTER 4

Jane M Powers
Speak with Confidence.
Sell with Authority

With decades of successful speaking and coaching, as well as real-life experience founding and running multi-million dollar businesses, Jane M Powers appreciates that success is truly about the power of your message. Entrepreneurs hire Jane to speak with confidence and sell with authority, so that they can generate a sustainable sales funnel to easily identify, capture, and close on ideal clients. With nearly thirty years of sales success as a corporate executive and entrepreneur, she brings everything any entrepreneur needs to take advantage of the most powerful marketing tool around—speaking, whether to one or one thousand!

Sample of Accomplishments after Publishing
Speak with Confidence. Sell with Authority

- Sold 250 books on the first day of launching the book.

- Has increased Jane's credibility and authority as a speaker. She now uses the book as a valuable prop on stage.

- Within three months of the book's launch, Jane can easily attribute at least a $50,000 increase in revenue for her own business.

Jane's Insider Secrets for First-Time Authors

I was not prepared for what writing my book *Speak with Confidence. Sell with Authority* (April 2018) kicked up for me. It awakened every inch of me. I found a voice for everything I was thinking, doing, saying, or experiencing at the time: "I'm not enough. I'm unworthy. I don't want to shine. I don't want the attention. I am an imposter. What if it's not really good?"

If you have any of those self-doubts humming along in your system, when you start writing your book, they will say, "Here we come!" For me, they sure came to the surface to be revealed and healed—AGAIN. I had no clue that would happen when I started writing a book. I found I had to heal from things I thought were complete for me.

Writing a book is an emotional awakening of everything. Prepare yourself!

Laura warned me this turmoil would happen, especially during the re-writing process. She said I would hate it. "There will be an emotional shift in you," she told me. But I never realized what that was going to look like. I would think, "I am done." And then she or her editor would give the manuscript back to me and say, "Here are eighty-two more things you have to do!" I would think, "Oh, God!" That was the worst! I wish I had prepared myself for the number of inevitable re-writes. I definitely experienced an emotional shift, but in the end, I'm glad I put in all that effort because my book has gotten results.

To save yourself time, money, and frustration, be consistent and disciplined about writing.

I wish I had been consistent and disciplined about writing. I would write for a while but then have long periods of time that I didn't write. By doing it that way, I would forget what I wrote and end up writing the same thing I'd already written! This happened over and over again. I kept repeating myself.

When Laura or my editor got ahold of my manuscript, they kept noting they had "read this before," which was frustrating for me. I would get my manuscript back and think, "Oh, come on!" But then I saw they were right, and it was bad! I'd tell them, "Well, it must have been a really good idea, or I wouldn't have kept writing it!" But this repetition caused a lot of wasted time and upset, so I wish I wouldn't have started and stopped so much.

Your book takes more than you might realize to get it out into the world—prepare early on and reach out for help.

I wish I had thought about the logistics of writing a book. When I should have reached out for more support from Laura, my writing coach, I avoided her instead (so I wouldn't have to do my writing).

I also wish I had known more about what it takes to launch a book and get it out into the world. Laura informed me, but I didn't get things together as soon as I would now. For example, I would have looked for promotional partners a lot earlier than a couple weeks before the actual launch date. I just didn't take the launch process seriously soon enough. In my opinion, affiliate partners are what it takes to become a bestselling author. I should have had a better system for preparing and not putting things off because it would have been a lot easier on myself and everyone else on my team.

I read some statistics recently that were very interesting. On average, 600,000 to a million books are written each year just in the United States. People will sell 250 of their books, but in a lifetime, they will sell 3,000 of their books. Peacock Proud Press's book launch system is defying the odds because I sold 250 books in just one day.

If you're a business owner, your book is about opening doors and closing deals.

I have a good business, and I've always wanted to write a book but never took the time to do it until I met Laura. If you are a business owner, understand that your book alone is not what will make you money. In other words, selling copies of your book is not going to make you rich. Instead, your book is a tool for building your business. Use it to open doors and close deals. It will generate results for you and your business in every way.

Hire the "right" team, not just "a" team to help you with your book.

Your book gives you more credibility and exposure. Although even me, a sales and business building expert, never really imagined a book would give me more than what I already had—but it has. So it's really important your book is great. My book would not be the book it is now without a team of support to leverage my business. You must, however, hire the "right" team, not just "a" team to help you write, publish, and launch your book.

How to Contact Jane M Powers

Website

janempowers.com

Let's Talk Impact – Annual Live Event

letstalkimpact.com

Social Media

facebook.com/JaneMPowers

linkedin.com/in/jane-m-powers

instagram.com/janempowers

twitter.com/janempowers

Email

jane@janempowers.com

CHAPTER 5

Lindsey Schwartz
Powerhouse Woman

Lindsey Schwartz is an Arizona-based, Wisconsin-born wellness entrepreneur, bestselling author, and founder of the annual Powerhouse Women Event in Scottsdale, Arizona. At age twenty-six, Lindsey started her first business part-time and over the next several years became an accomplished fitness athlete, full-time entrepreneur, speaker, and author. Lindsey's passion is to help women get out of their own way and confidently go after their big ideas and big dreams.

Sample of Accomplishments after Publishing *Powerhouse Woman*

- Invited to speak at Fitposium, a prestigious fitness conference and was awarded the 2017 Fitpreneur of the Year.

- Asked to become an Ambassador for Lululemon, a major fitness brand.

- Organized and established the annual Powerhouse Women event in Scottsdale, Arizona with one hundred participants in year one and two hundred participants in year two.

Lindsey's Insider Secrets for First-Time Authors

When I published my book, *Powerhouse Woman: How to Get Out of Your Own Way, Fulfill Your Unique Purpose, and Live a Powerful Life* (April 2017) I was a first-time author and an unlikely one at that. Although I had had a health and fitness blog for three years, I only published an average of one new blog article per year! You read that correctly. I had exactly three articles on my blog, and I'm pretty certain my mom was the only person who actually read them (Thanks, Mom!). Saying I didn't consider myself a writer is an understatement.

Despite the odds, I did write and publish a well-received book. I can also say with confidence that writing a book was one of the best experiences of my adult life. However, when I look back at the journey to becoming a published, bestselling author, there are a few things I wish someone had told me before I started.

Your book may never feel "finished."

When I finished writing the first draft of my manuscript, I wrestled with an unsettling feeling that it wasn't quite finished. No matter how many edits I made, I found new sections of the book that I wanted to improve. The feeling that the book wasn't perfect or "finished" almost kept me from publishing it altogether.

Here is what I know now: writing a book is a giant personal growth journey. The book I would write today would be different from the one I wrote last year. And that's okay. I think it's actually quite normal. When you undergo any kind of growth, your thoughts and ideas will naturally grow and evolve as you do. At some point, you must allow the book to be finished and then publish it for the world to read in order to clear space in your mind for new content to come through (your next book!).

You will probably want to quit at some point.

I've been there! Wanting to quit and not finish your book could show up in a variety of ways. For me, the biggest roadblocks were carving out uninterrupted time to write, battling through writer's block, feeling insecure about what others might think of the book (or me), and fearing deeply that other people were already writing about these same topics and were doing a much better job. If you've felt any of these things, you are not alone.

Deciding to write a book (or stepping out of your comfort zone for any reason) is an invitation for resistance to show up. Resistance isn't a bad thing; it just means you have an opportunity to grow. When you find yourself in the grip of resistance (doubts, fears, excuses), quitting will seem like a perfectly logical and valid choice.

My best advice for anyone wrestling with resistance is to remember that your book and your message are not actually about YOU. They are 100 percent about who you are going to serve.

When I took the focus off myself and, instead, thought about the women that I truly wanted to impact with my message, this focus helped me move through my resistance. You, too, will want to move through any resistance you're experiencing as quickly as possible because your biggest breakthroughs are typically waiting for you on the other side of your reasons to quit.

The blessings will far outweigh any obstacles.

No matter how much discomfort I had to work through to finish and publish my book, I would do it all again in a heartbeat, knowing now all the blessings waiting for me and my readers on the other side. In fact, the benefits I've experienced as a direct result of publishing my book have been incredible—everything from being invited to speak at events, to hosting my own Powerhouse Women's Event, to becoming an ambassador for Lululemon (my favorite apparel company), and recently at a fitness conference, being named "FitPreneur of the Year." I had NO idea that publishing a book would open up this many new opportunities for me.

If you have the slightest feeling that your message is meant to be shared in a book, do it! You may just surprise yourself with what you're capable of. And I can guarantee you'll positively impact a lot of other people in the process.

How to Contact Lindsey Schwartz

Website

lindseyschwartz.com

Powerhouse Women Event – Annual Live Event

Powerhousewomen.event

Social Media

Instagram.com/lovelindsfit

facebook.com/lindseymarieschwartz

Email

Powerhousewomenevent@gmail.com

PART II: BONUS

Information and Guidance from Experts

CHAPTER 6

Three Big Barriers to Writing a Bestselling Book

If you haven't written and published the book you've always wanted to write, it might be because you've been engaging in one of three big barriers to writing a bestselling book: dabbling, dawdling, or dashing. See if you recognize yourself in any of the following three problem scenarios and learn the simple solution to fulfill your book writing dream.

Dabble: (1) to immerse one's hands or feet partially in water and move them around gently (splash, dip, paddle,) or (2) to take part in an activity in a casual or superficial way.

A dabbling problem looks like you've been thinking about writing a book (or several books) off and on for years. Sometimes, you get casual feedback about your book ideas from friends or family, but you don't want too many people to know you're thinking about writing a book. Dabbling could also look like a stack of notes or fragments of documents you plan to use for your book. If you're a dabbler, you might honestly fear the time and effort you suspect it will take to get a book written, published, and marketed. You're waiting for just the right moment to really begin the process. In theory, you like the idea of having written a book, but you're just dabbling. You've only put your hands and feet in the writing water; your t-shirt and shorts are still dry.

Stop Dabbling and Commit

The solution to dabbling is to pull on your swimsuit and dive in the deep end of the pool. In other words, fully commit to invest the time and money it's going to take to write and publish a great book. This might include putting yourself in a writing program with a writing group, or hiring a writing coach and/or an editor. Eventually, you'll also need a book designer, publisher, and marketing plan. But if you keep dabbling around and avoid jumping in the water, you'll never finish your book.

Dawdle: (1) to waste time, be slow, (2) to move slowly and idly (amble, stroll, trail).

A dawdling problem is different from, but related to, dabbling. If you're dawdling, you've actually started writing your book. Congratulations! You might even have a couple of chapters written, but you lack direction. Trouble is, you're trying to do it all on your own. You think that's how books are written, and you have little to no idea about how to publish a book. So you slow the whole process down wondering what to do next. You probably haven't established a writing habit, either, so you're barely producing any writing on a regular basis. But you tell yourself going slowly is okay. You're writing a book after all. There's no hurry and you have other priorities. It's alright to stroll along for a few years. Your book will get finished eventually.

Stop Dawdling and Make a Plan

The solution to dawdling is to make a strategic plan, hopefully inside a book writing program or with a book writing and publishing expert. Investing in professionals will force you to set specific goals and deadlines for your book writing journey. You'll develop and stick to a writing habit. Having professionals in place will motivate you to make a difference for yourself and your readers because you've taken the plunge and invested in the support any expert needs to properly write, publish, and market a book.

Dash: (1) to run or travel somewhere in a great hurry, (2) to strike or fling somewhere with great force, especially so as to have a destructive effect (hurl, smash, crash, slam, toss, fling, pitch, cast, project, propel).

A dashing problem looks like writers who try to work as quickly through the process of writing a book as possible because they don't like the thoughts of revising and refining their ideas. They just want to free write (download their ideas from the universe), ask someone who's good with English to take a look at what they've written, and have that person tell them it sounds great!

If you're trying to dash your way through a book, you *might* be open to hiring an editor to clean up your brainstorming and get the grammar, spelling, and punctuation correct, but you don't really care that much about developing your ideas fully because developing your ideas takes too much time and effort. You want the book done and out the door making money or making a difference right away. If you're dashing along through a book, you probably also don't know who would want to read your book (wouldn't everybody?), but you believe your readership will sort itself out and each perfect reader will find your book like a soulmate.

Stop Dashing and Accept the Book Writing Process

The solution to dashing your way through a book is to accept that book writing is entering and preparing for a marathon, not a sprint. Just as your muscles and stamina must be built up over time to compete in a 26.2-mile race, the content of your book must be fleshed out and revised over time—at least six to nine months. No one would expect to enter a marathon with just a month's worth of training.

Writing a book also requires time for your ideas to percolate, be revised, and edited. Plus, the content needs to make sense to your reader and be well-structured. That takes time and effort too. You need to pace yourself to write a book. You also need to hire a team to travel beside you over the long miles, handing you bottles of Gatorade, cheering you on, and reminding you—when the going gets tough—why you wanted to write a book in the first place.

The Final Solution

If you care about the quality of your ideas, and if you care about influencing, motivating or engaging people's interest to buy, read, and even recommend your book, then you've got to stop dabbling, dawdling, and dashing. Bottom line, you've got to commit yourself, your time, and your money to write and publish a bestselling book.

Dr. Laura Bush published a ground-breaking book of literary research in Mormon women's autobiographies: Faithful Transgressions in the American West: Six Twentieth-Century Mormon Women's Autobiographical Acts *(Utah State University Press, 2004). She works as a writing coach, ghostwriter, editor, and publisher to help individuals and corporate leaders leave lasting legacies about their life and career.*

CHAPTER 7

Debunking the Myth of the Lone Writer

When you think of a "Writer," you probably think of a solitary person writing a book alone without much help. Somehow, you think, real writers are born to write. "It's easy for them," you say to yourself. "They read tons of books and always earned A's in English."

In your mind's eye, you see them happily typing away at their computer, hour after hour, with nothing to distract them from writing the brilliant book that few people are able or willing to write. Wrong!

Just read the acknowledgments page of any good book.

You'll see a long list of people who researched, provided guidance, gave feedback, edited, and otherwise supported an author's success.

While there *might* be an occasional genius that miraculously channels words onto a page without any angst or revision, the majority of writers, myself included, get our articles, our blogs, and our books written by working with others, especially when the going gets tough. And any time you write a book, the going will get tough.

Good book writing is not a sprint.

It's at least a half marathon that takes time and requires skillful planning. You deserve a good coach and a team of supporters who have run and won this kind of race before. They'll be cheering you on, handing you Gatorade, and helping you pace yourself all along the way.

In other words, collaborating with professionals and non-professionals alike is how books actually get written, finished, polished, and published.

Five Ways to Get Help Writing Your Book:

1. Find a writing partner.

This person should be someone you can trust to give you frank but supportive feedback, especially during the development and drafting phases of your writing. A writing partner can also serve double duty as an accountability partner.

My twin sister, Sarah, is my writing partner. I call her my "secret weapon" because after I've written a first draft of anything (like this chapter, for example), I become too close to my writing. I no longer see it as well from my reader's perspective. Conscientious writers will always try to anticipate what is unclear or missing for their audience, but having an actual reader give you specific feedback is invaluable. After Sarah reads one of my drafts, I ask her to tell me what she likes about it first. Then I'm better able to listen to what she says is confusing, underdeveloped, or poorly worded.

2. Join a writing group.

A writing group works much like a writing partner. The advantage is you gain two or more people's constructive and sometimes differing feedback. Although you as the author have the final say about your writing, when you hear similar comments from several readers, you should take their perspective into account and be grateful they're giving you access to your blind spots.

The easiest way to find a writing group is by searching for a Meetup or checking bulletin boards at local coffee shops, colleges, and libraries. If you can't find a group that fits your needs, consider forming one of your own with friends, colleagues, or family members interested in writing books themselves.

You can meet regularly in person or online using technology tools such as Google Docs, a private Facebook group, Skype, or Zoom (my favorite group conferencing software). You can also search for cost-effective group writing programs online. Webinars and short online courses can be a relatively economical way of joining a type of writing group where members are financially invested in each writer's success and where a qualified writing professional facilitates the group's meetings.

3. Hire a writing coach.

When I wanted to take my tennis game to the next level, I hired a tennis coach. Working with her on the court every week—first in small group classes and then privately—improved my technique, expanded the number of ways I could hit the ball, and gave me new strategies for competing. My confidence soared! Similarly, a writing coach can help you develop and organize your ideas while keeping you energized and excited as you improve your writing and see your book unfold. A writing coach will also pace you through the challenging phases of your book writing process, holding you accountable for achieving your ultimate book-writing goal.

4. Hire a ghostwriter.

If you want to author a book, but you don't have enough time or motivation to write it yourself, you can hire a ghostwriter to do the writing for you. Generally, a ghostwriter will record and then transcribe interviews with you to capture your distinct voice, experience, and expertise. You can also provide your ghostwriter with anything you may have written yourself already. Then you'll respond to drafts of the manuscript to ensure the writing accurately represents you and your message.

5. Assume you'll need an editor.

Everyone who writes a quality book needs a copy editor and a proofreader. A copy editor checks sources, makes sure your manuscript flows logically, and corrects any mistakes in grammar, spelling, punctuation, citations, or typos. When your text goes through the book formatting process, a proofreader catches any final errors in your manuscript. Even a professional writer like me uses an editor for proofreading and quality control.

In addition to these five ways to get help writing your book, authors who want people to actually read their book will seek feedback and testimonials from other experts in their field. This is an important part of nurturing key relationships and building an audience of people interested in reading your book when it's launched.

So, if you thought you had to write a book alone, you don't. In fact, every successful author collaborates. I urge you to do the same!

Dr. Laura Bush *published a ground-breaking book of literary research in Mormon women's autobiographies:* Faithful Transgressions in the American West: Six Twentieth-Century Mormon Women's Autobiographical Acts *(Utah State University Press, 2004). She works as a writing coach, ghostwriter, editor, and publisher to help individuals and corporate leaders leave lasting legacies about their life and career.*

Writing an Autobiography that Leaves a Lasting Legacy

An "autobiography" or "legacy book" is a personal history you write for family members, friends, and sometimes colleagues, hoping to inspire and influence them with the legacy of your personal life and career. At its best, your life story will impart your values and wisdom in a way that inspires, teaches, and leads those who come after you. Rather than a plodding story about when and where you were born, which schools you attended, and what degrees you earned or positions you've held, a great legacy book will delve into your dreams and reactions, emotions and personality. Written well, it will reveal not just your triumphs and joys, but your fears and insecurities, failures and foibles. Wrapped in authentic stories, descriptive details, and engaging dialogue, your legacy book can be one of the greatest gifts you ever give to your loved ones, friends, and peers or those you have mentored.

Start by Creating a Life Map

One way to start writing your legacy book is to draw a timeline of important events on a long roll of paper that will become a map of your life journey. Ideally, this paper can remain rolled out in a safe place for you to return to again and again. Create your timeline with large, easy-to-read lettering using a black marker or colored pens to distinguish key moments or turning points over each decade of your life. Jot notes to yourself about how you felt or what you learned from each life episode.

To expand your own view of your life and what's most notable to others, consider inviting family members, friends, or peers to jot down their own memories of events or interactions they recall having with you. Also, encourage them to write down their feelings or interpretation of those events. What did they learn from you or hear you say? Why did those things matter to them? You don't have to include everything other people mention on your life map. Just let them know you're gathering their ideas to help you remember and make decisions about what's most important.

Free Write and Chunk Material into Chapters

Once you've drafted your life map, you're ready to start the next phase of writing. Try not to censor your thoughts as you begin. Your first draft is for your eyes only. Simply free write about as many noteworthy events, places, and people as possible. Then chunk and organize that material into longer episodes or chapters about your life.

As an autobiographer, organizing your book can be challenging. Will you, for example, write chronologically from birth to your current age, or will you start in the present and then flashback to the past? What pictures will you include, if any and why? How will you transition from one period of your life to another? Rather than organize your legacy book chronologically, you might organize your life story based on topics, such as family, friends, career, hobbies, or places you've lived and traveled. You could also organize chapters based on life stories that exemplify your beliefs and values, such as "never give up," "be a lifelong learner," "defend others," "always negotiate," "stand up for a cause," "put family first," "plant gardens" (both literal and figurative), or "dance when no one is watching," etc.

Imagine Your Life as a Series of Scenes

While based on actual events from your life, experts in the field of autobiography consider life writing "creative nonfiction." In other words, to make a book engaging for readers, autobiographers write stories from their life just as they would create scenes for a movie, a play, or a novel. You, too, can simply imagine weaving together a series of key scenes from your life to become one coherent life story. At the very least, each scene will have a plot (what happened), a setting (the location or context), and characters (including you), who sometimes talk with each other (indirectly or directly, using dialogue).

Make Your Writing Vivid and Interpretive

To keep people reading, appeal to their five senses, ensuring each scene is vivid. Help readers see, touch, taste, smell, and hear what has happened to you and why that experience was important or how it shaped your choices in life. To help jog your memory for details, read old letters, email messages, social media posts, or a journal, if you kept one. Work to capture the personalities of those who nurtured, influenced, and spent the most time with you by including descriptions of specific clothing or jewelry they wore, how they walked, or what they did or said that impacted you and why.

Notice how the specificity of writing in the following excerpt from a published legacy book makes you feel like you are living this man's memories about loss:

> *I arrive back at my car, now as hot and dusty as I am. I long for the icy air-conditioning and a cold drink from my thermos. But I'm reluctant to leave. I keep looking around for something, as though I have lost something or left something behind. I know I may not be able to return, and truthfully, there is nothing to return to. It's just a dot on a map, a wide place in the road. I realize Metropolis is a*

> *metaphor for all that is dear to me—a sense*
> *of home, of family, of being at one with my*
> *people. A part of me is still here—will always*
> *be here. Dust clouds billow behind me as I*
> *drive away.*

Personal reflections and interpretations like this one provide life-like scenes that readers can identify with and learn from. Who hasn't been scorched by the heat of a day and been grateful for something cold to drink? What person hasn't felt grief over the loss of some place, some thing, or some one? Doesn't it always provide comfort knowing you're not alone? Your autobiography can provide your intended readers that type of comfort and courage, knowing that you, too, a real person, has survived and even thrived, after loss.

Decide What's Important or Not

One of the toughest things about writing an autobiography or legacy book is sifting through what's important and what's not. To make the most impact, the stories you tell and scenes you create about your life should be structured around a cohesive theme or overall message you want to share. Early on in your writing process, consider hiring a professional writing coach or editor who is practiced at storytelling and making tough decisions about which stories are important versus which stories are trivial (or maybe even boring) and need to go. You can also ask a friend or peer you trust to give you honest feedback about your manuscript. Then tell yourself, "Less is more" and dare to start writing your legacy book today!

Dr. Laura Bush published a ground-breaking book of literary research in Mormon women's autobiographies: Faithful Transgressions in the American West: Six Twentieth-Century Mormon Women's Autobiographical Acts *(Utah State University Press, 2004). She works as a writing coach, ghostwriter, editor, and publisher to help individuals and corporate leaders leave lasting legacies about their life and career.*

Evelyn Jeffries has written and edited numerous publications over her career. Currently, she has edited over twenty books for Utah and Arizona entrepreneurs, authors, and autobiographers. She also serves as a volunteer editor for the LDS Church History Department.

CHAPTER 9

Choosing the
Best Transcription Services

One strategy for getting your book written is "talking" your ideas into your phone or a digital recorder and then having that recording transcribed. For entrepreneurs on-the-go or for those who don't type quickly, capturing your expertise digitally and then transcribing those recordings for yourself can be a viable option. Besides saving you money, transcribing your own recordings as part of your writing process will ensure you know your material inside and out.

Transcribing your own recordings, however, can be difficult and tedious. If you don't have the proper ergonomic set-up, it can take a toll on you physically. If you're a busy professional, it's also not likely the best use of your time. For a single project, it might make sense. But for an entire book, or as a standard component of your business process, hiring a professional transcriber can actually save you time and make you more money in the long run.

Nearly thirty years ago when I started offering transcription services—creating a typed document from a recording—I was capturing recordings from cassette tapes that customers sent me through the mail. Then I would send the transcripts back by Federal Express. Obviously, it was a different era.

Today, almost everything gets recorded digitally. My clients upload their recordings to my website, and I send my work back to them as an e-mail attachment. In my field, transcribers often use software programs such as Express Scribe and Inqscribe to do their work. In some cases, speech recognition software is now also a viable option.

Consider the benefits and drawbacks of the following three options for getting your project transcribed:

Use Speech Recognition Software

Over the years, the technology for recognizing and then automatically typing someone's speaking as she or he speaks has dramatically improved. Using a program such as Dragon Naturally Speaking can also help you avoid the physical stress from extensive typing. However, this technology works best if the software is trained to transcribe just one voice. You will also need to say all the punctuation during your dictation (or add punctuation later), which can be cumbersome and time *consuming* rather than time *saving*.

Hire A Large Transcription Company

Rates of large company's like rev are generally cheaper. They can also often offer a faster turnaround time. But do you feel okay about a person you have not personally screened transcribing your confidential material? With a long-term project like a book, you also need to think about consistency. The skill rates of the transcribers in large companies can vary widely. Contractors for these companies mostly work at minimum wage. They have no time or incentive to focus on punctuation, spelling, or the context of your writing. If you need your work transcribed cheap and fast, this is your best option, but the quality of the transcription may suffer.

Hire A Professional Transcriber

While hiring a professional transcriber can be more expensive, most of the transcribers I know are also editors or have an editing background. This means you'll get back a transcript that is punctuated correctly and follows the standards of the Chicago Manual of Style. Professional transcribers like me can also individualize the format of your document to meet your needs. At my company, for no extra charge, I provide word lists of names and terms that I have researched and verified. I mark best-guessed words with time codes and can also insert time codes at the beginning of answers to interview questions, if that is helpful. I offer a table of contents that provides you a guide to subjects discussed in an interview. I also do not charge for "down time" in a recording. So, for example, I will not charge you for any chit chat, technical issues, or other moments in the recording that are outside of the scope of a recording of an interview. I mark these "down time" moments with time codes. All these features that professional transcribers offer can actually reduce your writing and editing time.

Knowing the advantages and disadvantages of each transcribing option should help you choose the best option for your writing project.

Wendy Ledger *owns* VoType Editorial and Transcription Services. *She earned her editing certification through the UC Berkeley Extension Profession Sequence in Editing program. She is also the author of two coming-of-age novels,* Joy Returns! *and* Kate and the Horses.

CHAPTER 10

Three Ways to Find Time to Write

One of the legitimate concerns people face when it comes to writing a book (or even a blog) is finding time to write. Believe it or not, as a well-published author, I can sympathize. I'm always writing or editing for my clients—that's my job! What often feels like a struggle, however, is finding time to do my *own* writing.

I've learned there are three things you can do to find time to write what really matters to you, especially when it comes to writing and finishing a book. At first glance, these three things might seem obvious. And in one sense, they are, but then . . . why don't you do them? Because you still haven't prioritized yourself and your writing.

Here are three things you can do right now to find time to write:

1. **Value What You Have to Say**. If you question the value of what you have to say (the legitimacy of your expertise or the importance of your life experience), you will always put off your writing. When you doubt the ideas and solutions you have to offer others, you

end up dealing with a project for work, cleaning your desk, or tackling whatever has climbed highest on your "to do" list, instead of writing. The minute you *really* believe, even a little bit, that you have something valuable to say that will help people, you will make the time to write.

2. **Determine What Time of Day Your Brain Thinks Best**. When you begin writing on any project (a book or a blog), it's best to allow yourself time to freewrite whatever comes to mind without censoring yourself. This is sometimes called content dumping. Ultimately, though, great writing is not just plopping words helter skelter on a page. You need to organize and develop your thoughts so they make sense to your reader. That type of intellectual work means you need focused time to think and write well. Ideally, then, you should identify the best hours during the day when your mind is rested, strong, and clear. For me, that's in the morning. If I must, I can write at night, but it's not much fun, and I'm easily inclined to put writing off when I'm tired.

3. **Block Out Writing Time Consistently throughout Your Week**. Once you've determined when your brain works best for focused thinking, block out at least one hour of time to write at that exact time. For me, blocking from 9:00 – 10:00 a.m. BEFORE I read email,

check social media, or do anything else works well for me. Sometimes I block out three hours in the morning to write. You get to choose what time works best for you and your brain. Then don't allow anything except a legitimate emergency to interfere with that time on your calendar. If you schedule and guard your time to write, you will write.

Once you consciously build a writing habit into your calendar, you'll also build the momentum and the confidence to keep writing. You won't keep putting it off. Neil Fiore, PhD, author of *The Now Habit*, says, "People don't procrastinate just to be ornery or because they're irrational. They procrastinate because it makes sense, given how vulnerable they feel to criticism, failure, and their own perfectionism."

Finding time to write can happen in an instant when you believe in yourself, even a little bit. As soon as you ignore your inner critic and any nagging fears about what other people might think or whether you're good enough to become the author of a book, finding time to write consistently becomes a breeze.

Dr. Laura Bush *published a ground-breaking book of literary research in Mormon women's autobiographies:* Faithful Transgressions in the American West: Six Twentieth-Century Mormon Women's Autobiographical Acts *(Utah State University Press, 2004). She works as a writing coach, ghostwriter, editor, and publisher to help individuals and corporate leaders leave lasting legacies about their life and career.*

CHAPTER 11

Is Your Editor a Friend or Foe?

If you've never worked hand-in-hand with an editor before, you may not know much about how the editing process works. You might also be afraid of what an editor will think about your writing. Will she be your friend or your foe?

Writers new to working with editors might picture them as people like your seventh-grade English teacher bent over papers, red pen in hand, gleefully marking up the page and silently assigning a low grade to your work. But great editors are not simply hell-bent grammarians who only focus on subject-verb agreement, vague pronouns, dangling modifiers, and the like.

Anonymous Versus Collaborative Editors

As a seasoned freelance editor who works with authors on everything from blog posts to books, I can tell you I want to be your friend, not your foe. Sure, if you go to an online editing mill, folks on the other end who don't know or care about you often just look at what you've written and have at it with little concern for your thoughts or feelings! The only thing these anonymous editors deal with is the writing itself. They have no relationship with you. What's more, the pay-per-word culture drives them to get it done and move on to the next manuscript as soon as possible. This impersonal process doesn't allow for much emotional investment or meaningful interaction with you as the writer.

In contrast, I see my role with authors as that of a collaborator. Great editors care deeply that your writing shines; they want to contribute to the quality of your writing and thinking beyond grammar, spelling, and punctuation. The best editors are very capable of doing so. Of course, as a technician their skill in copyediting is to help make your message clear, concise, consistent, and complete. This serves your readers so they don't have to labor through hard-to-read material that can confuse or distract from your message. However, there's even more value a great editor can offer.

Technical and Developmental Support

Typically, when I sign on to a writing project, I intend to develop an ongoing relationship with you as a writer. I will not only improve the technical aspects of your writing, I will also advise and empower you to improve the structure and development of your manuscript, offering you plenty of positive feedback along the way. Since I take the place of your reader, if something doesn't make sense to me (there's an obvious gap or confusion), my job is to identify areas like this so you can fill in what's missing or clarify your ideas.

As necessary, I will also ask you questions about your meaning, your tone, or your style. Occasionally, I may ask you to discuss or further develop a particular aspect of your manuscript. On some points, I may be adamant; on others, I may only make a suggestion or offer an opinion. After all, the writing is ultimately your work. Even grammar rules have gray areas. But an initial back-and-forth process between us enables me to learn what you might accept or reject using the beloved "track changes" feature of MS Word. This back and forth allows me to better understand your perspective as we move forward. It will also give you a better idea of things to watch for in your future writing.

Tough-Love Cheerleaders

Basically, my role as an editor requires a combination of tough love and cheerleading support. Sometimes, I will say it straight with what may seem like a critical voice to someone who feels their soft insides revealed and then poked on the page. But I aim to frame my comments in a positive way so that you can hear them. Having a friendly relationship with you as a writer influences how I communicate with you and vice-versa.

Realize that great editors have a vested interest in making your work brilliant. After all, your published writing also reflects their editing abilities. In other words, the best editors are on your side! Relish their input and work with them as a partner and a supportive colleague so you can birth your very best creation.

---

*M. **Lisa Forner** is a freelance editor based in Phoenix, Arizona. Her editing experience spans several decades and ranges from blog posts to published books in business, education, consumer/lifestyle, and government arenas.*

CHAPTER 12

Why You, Too, Are Good Enough to Write Your Book

During a C-SPAN panel discussion in 1997, journalist and intellectual Christopher Hitchens (1949-2011) said, "Everyone has a book inside them." As an aspiring author, I was fortunate that I never knew he also said, "in most cases, that's exactly where it should remain."

Before publishing my book, *When Death Comes Knocking for Your Patients*, if I had known Hitchens' full opinion, I might have kept my stories and my words of wisdom for nurses and other palliative caregivers locked away inside me for eternity. As an oncology nurse of over thirty years, I had enough doubts about my ability to write a book without adding Hitchens' so-called words of wisdom to my own internal dialogue, which tried to convince me I was "not good enough" and "No one will be interested in what I have to say."

Fortunately, my experience of writing and publishing a book has shown me that my words can make a difference. I am an expert in my own experiences as an oncology nurse and palliative caregiver, helping individuals and their families deal with end of life diagnoses. The positive feedback I have gotten from readers has had me realize that my book has already made a difference and will continue to do so in several ways.

First, since publishing my book in September 2017, one of the largest schools of nursing in Arizona, Pima Medical Institute, has ordered fifty copies for their senior nursing students. This means that *When Death Comes Knocking for Your Patient: A Guide for Nurses and Palliative Caregivers* will become a valuable resource for these future nurses as they commit to quality patient care. My book also has the potential to be adopted as part of other national and international nursing curriculums. This unexpected outcome would never have happened if I had not had the courage to write and publish my book.

Second, I'm leaving a legacy of my life's work, especially for other caregivers. When I began writing, I thought I had wanted to make a difference for those who were dying. Then I realized I didn't know what it was like being diagnosed with a terminal illness. I have never faced cancer myself. However, I can empower cancer patients' journey by empowering those who take care of them at their bedside.

Third, I've learned I *am* a good writer, and I didn't know that before publishing my book. Hundreds of people (strangers, friends, family, and colleagues) have reached out to tell me how much my writing has touched them and how moved they are by my book. I still can't hear their praise enough to really get it.

But now, as a semi-retired nurse, when I answer the question on applications, "What's your occupation?" I write, "I am an author and a registered nurse working casually."

Although Christopher Hitchens did not believe the books within many of us can make a difference given the opportunity to put our thoughts onto paper, I'm happy I did not listen to his advice. Becoming a published author has been the key to unlocking opportunities for me to speak, teach, and ensure new nurses have a resource to empower them under difficult situations and offer high quality care to cancer patients and their families.

At the end of my own life, I hope the person taking care of me will have read my book, or one like it, so that they can connect with me, ensuring my transition from this life to the next is powerful and dignified. In other words, I want someone just like me to take care of me. That very well could be because someone read my book.

Bestselling author **Meina J. Dubetz**, *is a Registered Nurse with certifications in oncology and gerontology. She lives in Calgary, Alberta Canada and spends her winters near Casa Grande, Arizona. Find out more about Meina and her books at meinadubetz.com*

CHAPTER 13

Financing Your Writing

I know sometimes it's tough to deal with the challenges of feeling like you don't have enough money to do the things you really want: take a vacation, buy a new car, or even start your own business. I have spent many years as a business coach training people around sales and money conversations. Over those years, I've heard far too many times, "I don't have the money," only to come to the realization that people will find a way to afford what they truly desire. In other words, you can and *will* find the money to pay for what you love, including writing a book.

I'm sure it isn't just me. I'm sure you, too, have got something to say to the world (or you wouldn't be reading this book). The greatest advice I can give you is this: when you're ready to write your book, do it right the first time. Hire the best and invest in support to write and publish a really good book. I'm sure I don't need to tell you that's going to cost money. At the very least, you'll need to purchase two ISBNs (one for the print and one for the e-book), you'll need to pay for the book to be edited, and if you're smart, you'll also make sure to have the interior and cover of the book designed by a professional book designer.

Readers DO judge a book by its cover, and if you want your book to sell (as I'm sure you do), investing in the editing, design, marketing, and promotion of your book is a no brainer.

So how do you finance your writing, pay your bills, and finish your book? Here are five places to start.

1. **The easiest trick to get money is apply for a 0% interest card for twelve to twenty months and finance your own book.**

    That's a free loan of money and for almost two years in some cases. I've done this myself in the past to build my own business. At one time, I had a 0% card for $35,000, $33,000, and $28,000 all at the same time. The payments were as low as $300 per month. This type of self-financing leverages you enough time to gain capital. It's a smart way to leverage someone else's money.

2. **Start a *Go Fund Me*, *Kickstarter*, or *Smashfund* Campaign.**

    I have used Smashfund to raise money for nonprofits at my three-day "Let's Talk Impact" live events, which you should attend. The three campaigning systems are very similar. I like Smashfund because it's free, for now, and you keep one hundred percent of the money you receive. You simply create an account and send out your campaign to supporters. I recommend donating half of what you earn to a charity and keep the rest for your book.

3. **Sell your existing programs and services.**

    If you're writing a book, you're a subject matter expert who can turn your expert content into a workshop, a retreat, or an online program that you can sell, even if you don't have the book out yet. A great way to put on a cost-effective workshop is to have a friend host it for you. You can couple it with a wine tasting party. You deliver the content of your book in a workshop format as people enjoy the different wines. You can provide snacks and desserts. Make sure you charge a fee for the workshop and PRE-sell your book.

4. **If you're on a mission to help other people with your book, you can do a fundraiser to get the word out and/or ask for sponsorships.**

    The fundraiser might be a dance-a-thon, a walk-a-thon, a bake sale, or a fundraising dinner. You can invite a small group of friends and family or go all out and invite anyone and everyone. People love to help, and they also love a party. Again, motivate others to give by donating a portion of the proceeds to a related cause. Depending on the subject matter of the book, you could also ask for sponsors. Half the money goes to charity and half goes to the awareness book. You can even name the sponsors in your book.

5. **Ask and ask again!**

   I have clients that are afraid to ask their spouse or loved ones for money. I always recommend having a structured plan in hand before you begin such a conversation. For example, you can create a payment plan that includes a small monthly interest. You might offer them a 2–3% interest payment. They can't even get that interest rate at a bank! Establish manageable payment terms that are realistic for you. I have clients borrow money from their loved ones and agree to start paying the loan after six months, but not to exceed twenty-one months. The good news is you will write your book and then go make some money off it, whether you are selling products, services, or just books.

Ultimately, you've got to get yourself into the mindset of possibility. I would take a moment and ask yourself, "What can I do to find the money to finance my book?" Then turn over every rock so you have the financial means to express yourself in one of the most credibility-building ways possible—a book. Finally, remember that the money excuse for not writing a book may be just that—an excuse. Never let anything stand in your way, especially money. Go out, find the money, and get writing that book!

__Jane M Powers__ has over thirty years of sales success as a corporate executive, entrepreneur, international speaker, and coach, including her real-life experience founding and running multi-million dollar businesses. Using her straight forward, big-hearted style, Jane empowers thousands to transform their message to money. Find out more about Jane at janempowers.com.

CHAPTER 14

Are You Ready to Audiobook?

More and more nonfiction authors are recognizing the incredible potential audiobooks offer their business. Eager entrepreneurs, however, may dive in headfirst without giving sufficient forethought into how this unique tool can best be leveraged.

Audiobooks are the fastest-growing sector of the entire publishing industry. The Association of American Publishers show audiobook downloads up by 31.1 percent from 2015 to 2016—part of a five-year trend, and counting. One factor that contributes to this exponential increase in audiobook readership is accessibility—audiobooks are now available through our phones, laptops, and tablets. There's no barrier to where and when we can listen. The cost of audiobook production has also dropped dramatically—nearly 50 percent since 2009.

As a nonfiction audiobook publishing specialist, I see critical mistakes and bottom-line opportunities overlooked time and again. If you are an author keen on taking advantage of this booming advancement in publishing—and you have every reason to be—pay attention to these five factors that will make sure your audiobook is the asset you want it to be and a fabulous tool to grow your audience, influence, and income.

1. Don't Voice Your Own Book (unless…)

One of the most frequently asked questions I receive is, "Should I narrate my own book, or work with a narrator?" That is the wrong question to ask. What you really want answered is the question, "Is there any *advantage* to narrating the book myself?" Most often, the answer is no. Here's why:

Audiobook Creation Exchange (ACX) reports that it takes an average of 6.2 hours of production time for a professional narrator and editor to create one hour of finished audio. That means that an average nonfiction book of 60,000 words requires twenty-five to thirty hours of production time—for an experienced professional. Even if you're an experienced public speaker or podcaster, the skill set for audiobook narration is distinct. In addition to specialized voice training and having to learn microphone and breathing technique, consider the time and expense for a home recording studio setup or rental time in a recording studio. All in all, you can reasonably expect to triple your time investment or more.

Instead, your audiobook could be professionally produced at a reasonable cost and delivered to the world with ease in about 6 weeks. You could be reaping the benefits and leveraging this asset *like a boss*, rather than spending your time and money going through a learning curve you simply don't need to go through.

There is, however, an exception to this rule. If you have a following in the millions who is used to you speaking on stages, on TED talks, or in other audio recordings—and you have built your platform and reputation around your unique voice and speaking qualities—then you may be a good candidate to voice your own audiobooks. Otherwise, ditch the temptation to try to save money—because you won't.

2. Know Your Rights

Don't fall prey to the amateur mistake of not knowing your audio rights. It is imperative that you understand the legalities of audiobook production, so that you can protect your intellectual and financial investments.

If you're planning to work with a publisher, this information is absolute gold for you as you negotiate your contract. Many authors sign their audio rights away without even knowing it— they find out after the fact that an audiobook version of their print book has been created, and worse yet, they won't receive reasonable royalties for the sales of that audiobook. With the rise in audiobook popularity, lack of attention to this detail can add up to substantial financial loss.

3. Collect Bounties

Audible, Amazon, and iTunes have a common back end for self-published authors to produce audiobooks. It's called ACX. com (Audiobook Creation Exchange). If you hold the rights to your audiobook and distribute your audiobook through ACX. com, you are eligible to earn bounties.

A bounty is an additional type of earning paid to you when your book is the first purchase of a new Audible member. For each bounty earned, you receive $50. Unfortunately, ACX is only available to authors living in the U.S. or U.K., but a good audiobook publisher can help other international authors take advantage of this opportunity as well as self-publishing royalty rates, adding significant income to your bottom line.

4. Leverage Your Launch

There are two "right" ways to launch an audiobook. In one scenario, your previously launched print or digital book is given new life by being turned into an audiobook format.

This strategy gives you the ability to have an entirely new product launch without having to create any new content. If your content needs a little updating, then pairing an "anniversary edition" or "second edition" of your book with an audiobook version is a fantastic option.

Second, if you're in the process of getting ready to publish a new book, having an audiobook version will extend the life of your launch. To have a powerful launch, you want to reach as many people for as long as possible. Releasing your audiobook two to twelve weeks following your initial book release allows you to keep the momentum and excitement going—with minimal changes to your social media and email content.

5. Build a Podcast Tour

In today's high-tech publishing world, it's no secret that in-person book tours are not a cost or time-effective means to connecting with your market. Blog book tours have been an alternative practice for several years now, but a lesser-known opportunity exists via podcast tours.

A podcast is a downloadable, online radio show—a thriving platform for effectively broadcasting your brand. There are now nearly 60 million people in the U.S. alone listening to podcasts every month; this presents a giant opportunity for you to engage with potential readers—if they listen to podcasts, they likely also listen to audiobooks.

Connect with the hosts of podcast shows that intersect with your target market and arrange to be a guest expert on their shows. Conduct a book reading, answer insider questions about the subject matter, and share how listeners can access further information about your title and services.

To *really* be a boss, send a short clip of your audiobook to the podcast host in advance of your interview, and invite them to post the clip along with their Amazon affiliate link to your book and audiobook. The host can also include this link in his or her website copy (or "show notes," as they are known in podcasting) for your podcast episode. This strategy creates more rich content for the host, and an opportunity for both you and the host to benefit financially.

Work with the podcast host to have the show published during your initial launch window, and boom—you've successfully leveraged your audiobook to drive sales and initial rankings far beyond the level of a mere beginner.

Tina Dietz is the owner of StartSomething *Creative Business Solutions and an internationally acclaimed business consultant, audiobook publisher, podcast host and launch specialist, and professional speaker/ voice talent who has been featured in such outlets as ABC, Inc.com, Huffington Post, and Forbes.*

CHAPTER 15

Avoid Costly Mistakes: Know Your Publishing Options

There's never been a better time to publish your book. There's also never been a better time to make a lot of self-publishing mistakes.

To avoid the most costly mistakes, you should know the key differences between traditional versus self-publishing, including three different ways to self-publish. Knowing your options will help you choose the book publishing path that's right for you.

Traditional Publishing

The "Big Five" traditional publishing houses pay YOU to publish your book. This means they're paying for the rights to your content (i.e. intellectual property) and up to 80 percent of your royalties (i.e. profits). Think of traditional publishers as venture capitalists who need and want to make a substantial return on their investment to edit, design, publish, distribute, and promote your book. Just like any good VC, they publish authors that increase the odds they'll make money.

Massive competition in the publishing industry has led traditional publishers to gravitate toward well-established authors, public figures, or celebrities who already have thousands, if not millions of followers. That way, traditional publishers can count on these authors making them a profit.

If you're not a celebrity, but you *are* an excellent writer who is committed to publish traditionally (and beat the odds stacked against you), then you'll need to write a compelling query letter and/or book proposal that will command an editor's attention within three to five minutes. Gatekeeper editors at traditional publishing houses separate the wheat from the chaff very quickly. Even to get in the door, you will need a literary agent because traditional publishers no longer deal directly with authors. Your literary agent should have the expertise to identify the right publisher for your book, negotiate the best deal possible, and help you retain as many of your rights as possible.

Three Ways To Self-Publish

If you have an important life story, message, or expertise to share in a book, you can avoid the daunting roadblocks of traditional publishing by self-publishing in one of three ways: (1) Do It Yourself, (2) Vanity Book Publishing, or (3) Independent Book Publishing.

1. Do It Yourself

Kindle Direct Publishing or KDP, an Amazon company that merged with its former company CreateSpace, offers free tools to help you create your book cover, review your book's interior (the format of your print and ebook), and get useful feedback from readers before you start selling your book. With a KDP account, you'll be able to receive royalties and distribute your book through Amazon.

DIY self-publishing gives authors an affordable way to get their message out. But there's also the challenge of finding a good editor (if you use one at all), formatting your book correctly, designing an eye-catching cover, coming up with a great title, and writing persuasive back cover copy that sells your book. You also need to know details about an ISBN, LCCN, bar code, pricing, and more. Many people self-publish their book with relatively little professional assistance and feel satisfied with the process. Often, however, the book's content and cover reflect a do-it-yourself product.

The Value of Assisted Self-Publishing: If you're a business professional or someone who wants to stand confidently behind the value of your book, you should **not** publish your book without professional assistance. Your time is too valuable and a DIY book will not gain you the credibility you need. Instead, hire professionals to assist you through the book publishing, marketing, and distribution process. A professionally published book will help you establish your authority, maximize your influence as a thought leader, and leverage you and your book's success.

Although the line can seem blurry between two forms of assisted self-publishing ("vanity" or "independent" book publishing companies), you can tell the difference based on a few key factors. One caution though: how a publishing company refers to itself does not necessarily indicate which type of assisted self-publishing company they might be, nor the quality of services you will receive. Do your research.

2. Vanity Book Publishers (Assisted Self-Publishing)

Generally, vanity book publishers won't call themselves by this name, but they are referred to this way within the industry because they publish almost any manuscript, regardless of its quality, as long as an author pays them.

These self-publishing companies will assist you by providing editing, book design, book formatting, and even some marketing services. They often offer lower-cost publishing services because they focus on the quantity of book publishing contracts sold, not necessarily a book's excellence. Their business model depends on volume and a factory-like process to lower costs. They may also get certain rights to your book, but not make the release of your rights clear to you. You can get your rights back, but you will likely have to pay for them and that could become a struggle.

Do careful comparison research, talk to actual people at any publishing company to get a feel for their customer service, interview actual authors who have published with the company, and read the fine print.

3. Independent Book Publishers (Assisted Self-Publishing)

An independent book publisher is a hybrid between traditional and vanity book publishers. Like traditional publishers, independent book publishers are committed to the quality of the content and production (design, marketing, launch, and distribution) of your book. They know that self-publishing is challenging because you as an author don't know the steps to publish and launch a professional book that sells. Independent book publishers do that work for you, and you keep most or sometimes even all the rights and royalties to your book.

As a member of the Independent Book Publishers Association, our mission at Peacock Proud Press is to publish books that transform the lives of our authors and their readers. We offer three different publishing packages to meet the needs and budgets of our authors. We also want our authors to feel "peacock proud" of their book, so we adhere to the IBPA's

Industry Standards Checklist for a Professionally Published Book. This checklist is a great tool for anyone who wants to self-publish a professional quality book.

Regardless of which self-publishing path you choose, avoid wasting your time and money. Take time to do careful research to determine which path and which company are right for you.

Dr. Laura Bush *published a ground-breaking book of literary research in Mormon women's autobiographies:* Faithful Transgressions in the American West: Six Twentieth-Century Mormon Women's Autobiographical Acts *(Utah State University Press, 2004). She works as a writing coach, ghostwriter, editor, and publisher to help individuals and corporate leaders leave lasting legacies about their life and career.*

You Can Write and Publish Your Book, Too!

We hope the writing and publishing information and advice you got from these first-time authors and our experts at Peacock Proud Press will inform and motivate you to write the book of your dreams. Each of these first-time authors have fulfilled their dream to write, publish, and successfully promote their book and their message. They continue to do so today.

The valuable advice they offer other would-be authors comes straight from their own writing and publishing experience. They share how they both stumbled *and* succeeded throughout their writing, revising, and publishing process. Ultimately, these authors prevailed because they set a big-dream publishing goal and got the right support they needed to achieve that goal.

Publishing a well-received book is a big deal, and you can do it, too—if you're genuinely committed. Committing to a book means you're willing to invest the time and financial resources needed to write, publish, launch, and promote your book with the help of a supportive, skilled team.

When writing drafts of your manuscript, consider the sage advice of novelist, editor, and professor E.L. Doctorow, who says, "Writing is like driving at night in the fog. You can only see as far as your headlights, but you can make the whole trip that way."

To finish and publish your book, decide to turn on your headlights and make the journey through what might seem, at times, like an awful lot of fog. Why make the journey? Because we don't know any author who has regretted publishing a book, even if it makes a difference for just one person. And that one person could be YOU!

About Laura Bush, PhD

 Dr. Laura Bush is the Founder and CEO of Peacock Proud Press. Entrepreneurs, speakers, and coaches hire her to unleash the world class author in them because most have had a book stuck in them for years and are missing out on the financial benefits of increasing their visibility and differentiating themselves as an authority in their industry. She helps them get their book finished with confidence and ease, so they can establish their credibility and be seen as experts who make a bigger difference and a bigger income!

In 2012, Dr. Bush started her business after a twenty-year career as a faculty member teaching literature, composition, and business writing courses in person and online. She earned her PhD in English from Arizona State University, specializing in western American women's autobiography. Then she published her ground-breaking book of literary research in Mormon women's autobiographies: *Faithful Transgressions in the American West: Six Twentieth-Century Mormon Women's Autobiographical Acts* (Utah State University Press, 2004).

About Sarah Bush Lloyd

 Sarah Bush Lloyd earned an MEd in educational psychology and an MEd in school administration, as well as a BS in home economics, health, and vocational education from Brigham Young University. She worked as a principal, a guidance counselor, and a home economics and health teacher for over twenty-five years in Utah public schools before retiring to begin part-time work as a writing assistant and associate coach at Peacock Proud Press. Sarah is a skilled writer and an expert cook with extraordinary organizing skills and an eye for great design.

Find Out More

peacockproud.com